Sis,
GET UP

You were never meant to stay down.

STEPHANIE P. GREEN
Licensed Psychotherapist

Book Design by - DreamEmpire Publishing

Cover Art by - Joyce Licorish– DreamEmpire Publishing

For author booking inquiries, contact:

DreamEmpire Publishing

(317)292-6927 | www.DreamEmpirePublishing.com

Printed in the United States of America

First Printing Edition, Summer 2025

ISBN Paperback: 979-8-9991915-1-9

ISBN Hardcover: 979-8-9991915-0-2

Copywritten with the Library of Congress Control ID: 1-14858942711

Contents

lonliness

"Loneliness is often unspoken—yet it whispers like a calm breeze and sometimes roars like a lion. Don't miss the self-discovery that comes with becoming one with yourself."

STEPHANIE P. GREEN

DEDICATION

• • •

Thank you, Jesus, for giving me the strength, power, and the Holy Spirit to walk in my calling. Thank you for keeping my mind and protecting my heart when there was no hope and when I could only see death. I am not a victim of my circumstances. I am God's chosen vessel, as nothing just happened to me; it happened FOR ME!

For My Grandmother

I dedicate this book to the Woman of God who reared me, believed in me, showed me Christ, demonstrated what unconditional love is, displayed inner power and strength, and taught me by example everything I needed to become the woman I am today: my grandmother, Rosa L. Tucker Kirby. I carry you in my spirit and will be forever grateful for your guidance, support, and unwavering love. I loved you then, now, and forever.

For My Son

To my son Zion, my energetic, tenacious, warm-hearted young man. When I look at you, I see myself. The spirit you carry, the heart you have, and your relentless drive reflect beyond infinity. You are destined for greatness, and I will be in your peripheral, loving, supporting, and encouraging you every step of the way.

There is only one Zion Zyli Green with the DNA you encompass. Therefore, complete the journey you have before you, be a light to others, while understanding that there is no greater love than being an instrument of love.

It will be you-against-you on this life's journey—conquer you. The Holy Spirit is your guide and the way to all truths.

> *"God is not a man, that he should lie; neither the son of man, that he should repent: hath he said, and shall he not do it? or hath he spoken, and shall he not make it good?"*
>
> — *Numbers* 23:19 *(KJV)*

forced

Sometimes you may have to be <u>forced</u> out; to be <u>forced</u> into purpose.

STEPHANIE P. GREEN

INTRODUCTION

• • •

I am not trying to reach a specific demographic, ethnicity, culture, or denomination with this book. Instead, my intention is to simply reach the heart. Because, I know that what comes from the heart reaches the heart. Every word written has been inspired and designed to elevate, build, empower, and ignite the power within you.

I often ask God, "Why did You give me the kind of heart You did?" Now, more than ever, I understand that it takes a heart of unconditional love to speak to the innermost sensitive parts of another human being. I genuinely love and care for people, a gift that has been within me since childhood. As an empath, I literally feel the pain, hurt, joy, and sorrow of others when I listen and simply by looking at them.

Let's be real: this thing called **LIFE** has a way of shifting us in ways we could never imagine. Nevertheless, it's our responsibility to decide how we perceive those shifts. If you are a Child of God, He reminds us in His Word, *"And we know [with great confidence] that God [who is deeply concerned about us] causes all things to work together [as a plan] for good for those who love God, to those who are called according to His plan and purpose."* — Romans 8:28 (AMP)

No matter what has happened, is happening, or will ever happen, it has all been divinely orchestrated by the Most High God to bring forth purpose—if we are walking in His Will. **SIS, Get Up**. You have the power within you to rise again.

As you read through these pages, I encourage you not to simply read the words, but to absorb, process, reflect, and receive them. You are hearing from a woman who has been to the darkest, lowest places—right up to the edge of death, in the grips of pain, grief, and sorrow. Yet, God is restoring, healing, and elevating me day by day. You, too, can, will, and shall make it through whatever you are enduring. I believe in you. I am standing with you in prayer, and confident that even now your season is shifting. **SIS, GET UP** and walk in your power and authority!

To write this book came at a great cost. The emotional and mental anguish endured throughout certain parts in my life have been inconceivable. For this reason I stand assured knowing If I can rise again so can you. Why? **Because...** *"I am you, and you are me."*

I encourage you to get the interactive workbook that accompanies this book so that you may have the full experience of engaging in the exercises designed to promote healing and impactful change.

PURPOSE

• • •

SIS, Get Up is for women who have experienced trauma, hardships, or setbacks they feel are irreconcilable or impossible to recover from. I am here as a voice of power, strength, and evidence that not only can you get back up, but you can get back up transformed and unrecognizable—through the power of God and your willingness to embrace the shift.

This book is for the broken-hearted, the burdened, the one who is suffering, those who have experienced any form of trauma , hurt, and for anyone who is just trying to find their way. I am here to speak life into you: **GET UP**. Give God something to work with to elevate you, evolve you, and form you into your greater purpose. But it will come with a requirement: being willing to say yes to the shift. That is what this book is all about.

peace
love & light

Peace calms, love
connects, and light
transforms-be the vessel
that carries all three.

STEPHANIE P. GREEN

MY STORY/ HOW I GOT HERE

• • •

"The pain that you've been feeling can't
compare to the joy that's coming."

— Romans 8:18

Life has a way of testing us in ways we could never anticipate. My story is one of love, heartbreak, betrayal, unexpected deaths and ultimately, redemption. I believed I was living "in truth"—until the cracks in that illusion shattered my reality. From deaths, to adultery, to emotional abuse, from deception to a complete unraveling of trust, I walked through fire. Yet, here I stand, stronger, wiser, and more determined to rise above the ashes.

This book is not just about the pain I endured; it's about how I got up. It's a testament to the power of faith, resilience, and choosing yourself when the world seems to crumble around you. My journey is shared here not to dwell on the past but to illuminate the path forward. For every woman who has felt broken, for every heart that has been shattered, know this: you can GET UP too.

While I am a Christian and my faith in God has been my anchor, I encourage you to lean on whatever Higher Power you connect with.

Ultimately, this is a story of universal truths—of hope, renewal, and the strength to rebuild.

Heartache has a way of making one question everything about themselves. The mental turmoil is beyond any words that can be expressed in human form which can also have the tendency to distort the mind. I knew I couldn't stay in that mindset any longer. At the time, I realized how the the minds of people who may contemplate suicide. I understand on a deeper level that suicidal thoughts aren't necessary about wanting to die—rather about wanting the pain to stop. I wanted the intrusive thoughts and the constant hurt to just go away. I didn't want to think about any of it anymore. You see, by this time, I taught about healing, preached about faith, and been a vessel of countless individuals healing, but the very thing I had helped so many others with I found myself not being able to help myself. I had never experienced this level of pain so deeply. Through my experience, I've learned an important lesson: True connection isn't about grand gestures; it's about the consistency of love and authenticity in actions.

Love, honesty, and mutual commitment is imperative in relationships. Proverbs 15:17 reminds us, "Better a small serving of vegetables with love than a fattened calf with hatred." The Bible speaks to the importance of loyalty in relationships in Matthew 19:6: "So they are no longer two, but one flesh. Therefore, what God has joined together, let no one separate." Without unity and commitment, even the strongest bonds can unravel.

When the divorce was finalized, I had to gain an understanding that healing requires boundaries. I learned to release the emotional ties that kept me tethered to the past, embracing Philippians 3:13-14: "But one thing I do: Forgetting what is behind and straining toward what is ahead, I press on toward the goal to win the prize for which God has called me heavenward in Christ Jesus."

Ultimately, this chapter of my life taught me the value of accountability, forgiveness, and moving forward. It reminded me that while I cannot control the actions of others, I have the power to choose how I respond, grow, and rise above. Letting go wasn't just about the past—it was about freeing myself to step into the life I was meant to live.

It wasn't just the end of my marriage that broke me—there were losses that compounded my grief. My beloved grandmother, the woman who reared me, passed away unexpectedly in her sleep. I had spoken with her the night before, followed by the murder of my brother just five months later. It felt like wave after wave of compound trauma, and I could hardly breathe. The stress of it all took a toll on my body—blood pressure spikes, heart monitors, insomnia and emotional breakdowns. I was at my breaking point. Dealing with business suffering due to being unable to work at times from mental distress, lost loved ones, failing health, and the collapse of my marriage—all at once. I didn't understand why this was happening.

But through all of that pain, something powerful happened: I began to rise. Slowly, piece by piece, I started placing my focus back on Jesus and learned how to really trust him and begin working on building myself back together. I realized that no one else could save me—I had to choose to save myself. I had to fight for my own healing, even when it felt like there was nothing left to fight for. And through that journey, I discovered that I was so much more than what I had endured. I was not defined by my pain or by the people who had hurt me.

Sis, Get Up isn't just a story about betrayal or loss—it's about the power of healing, resilience, and the journey toward self-love and rediscovery. In this book, I will walk you through some of the dark parts of my story and ways to healing without going too deep, keeping in mind the relationship that damaged me most happens to also be the relationship with my son's father. With that in mind, instead of harping on the past, I want to show you how, even in the midst of heartbreak and loss, we can rise stronger, wiser, and more empowered than ever.

Yes, I've been through the fire, but I didn't come out scorched. I came out refined. And if you're reading this, I believe that you too are on the brink of a breakthrough. Sis, it's time to get up. It's time to choose healing over hurt, love over loss, and freedom over fear. Your story doesn't end here—it begins now.

healing

Healing is not just
mending what hurt - it's
meeting the woman you
were always meant to be
beneath the wounds.

STEPHANIE P. GREEN

Chapter 1

HEALING THE WOUNDED SOUL

• • •

"And we know that in all things God works for the good of those who love Him, who have been called according to His purpose."

— *Romans 8:28*

It happened. Now what? That was the question I found myself facing as I sat in the aftermath of betrayal, pain, and loss. I am an exceptionally private person, someone who doesn't share personal matters unless I trust you completely—a trust so rare, I can count on one hand the people who have earned it. My belief has always been that what people don't know, they can't destroy. So, let them speculate.

I never imagined I would be this open, this vulnerable, exposing my wounds for the world to see. I had always believed in keeping my struggles private, in not giving anyone ammunition to ridicule or attack me. But as I reflect on the pain and grief I've endured, I remember saying, time and again, "God is going to get the glory out of this, and I'm going to help other women rise above their pain and sorrow." I said it, but I didn't understand the magnitude of what it would cost me—spiritually, mentally, emotionally, and physically. The mental turmoil, sleepless nights, moments of backsliding, financial loss, health scares, all of it was more than I could have ever anticipated.

The humiliation, the shame, the mental anguish—they gripped me so tightly that some days I didn't want to leave my home. Healing became not just a hope, but a lifeline. It was clear to me that the trajectory of my life depended on it. The level of trauma I was experiencing could manifest in devastating ways if I didn't address it. There's no escaping the need for healing. The more you try to avoid it, deny it, or run from it, the more it will spiral out of control.

Here's the reality: healing will force you to face the very things that caused your trauma, grief, and heartache. Whether it's the loss of a loved one, unresolved grief, a rebellious child, a sudden health diagnosis, childhood trauma, infidelity, division within the family, spiritual conflict, or a broken friendship, you must confront it. It may sound harsh, but it's the truth: **"It happened. Now what?"** That was the harshest reality I had to come to terms with. How long was I willing to let my suffering control my life?

No matter where you go, healing will follow you because wherever you are, there you are. Healing is the internal process of addressing a spiritual dis-ease, and until you inject the antidote, the consequences will continue to wreak havoc on your life. Healing works from the inside out, slowly rebuilding you piece by piece. What is in a man is certain to come out of a man. The representative of a man has a set timeframe to perform until the authenticity of who they really are reveals itself.

The sooner you accept who you are and face your pain, the sooner you'll be able to have the life you desire. This was when I learned—truly learned—how to trust God and depend solely on Him. I thought I had trusted Him before, but I quickly realized I hadn't. There were times when I relied on others for emotional support and sought someone as an anchor to embrace the fall. But, what do you do when that person is no longer there? I was forced to ask myself:

NOW WHAT?

This book will help guide you through the necessary journey of healing, and how to move on and figure out what is next in your life. Together, we'll explore how to face your pain, confront your trauma, and find the strength to rise again. Through some of my story, I hope to guide you on your very own path of healing and transformation, showing you that while it happened, there's so much more waiting for you on the other side. Healing is possible, and you deserve it.

allow

"You allow what you believe to be true no matter how dysfunctional it may be."

STEPHANIE P. GREEN

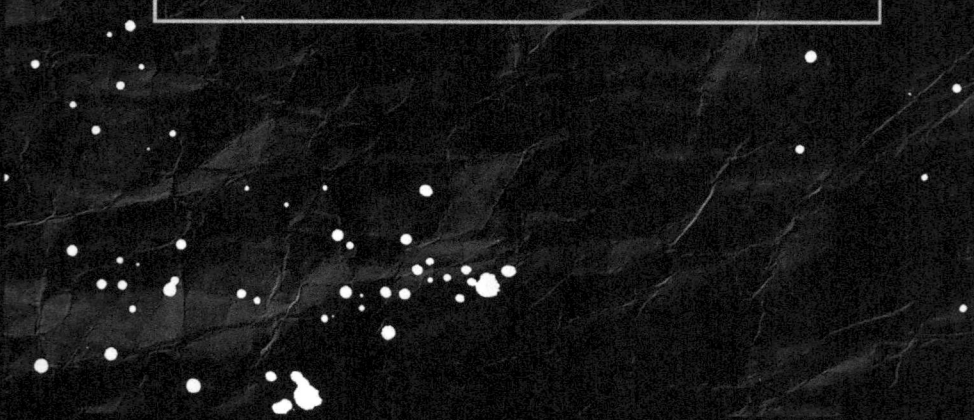

Chapter 2

I'M MESSED UP

• • •

"Being confident of this very thing, that he which hath begun a good work in you will perform it until the day of Jesus Christ:"

—Philippians 1:6

Let me start by saying, it does not matter how tumultuous, defeated, or—in your eyes—unfruitful life may have been or may appear to be currently. There is nothing, and I do mean nothing, that God is not able to work out for your good. "And we know that all things work together for good to them that love God, to them who are called according to his purpose." —Romans 8:28. In other words, it may not make sense now, but in due season, it will. Keep this in mind: things do not just happen to us; they happen for us, based on the lens through which we choose to view them.

I don't think there is anyone walking this earth who consciously says, "I want to stay bound, I want to feel pain, let me suffer more, I love the way this hurts me, give me more trauma." But that's exactly what happens when we refuse to face reality and won't admit to ourselves, "I'm messed up." The reality is that healing cannot begin until we honestly confront the truth of where we are and what we're dealing with. Denial is a powerful force, and it can keep us stuck—afraid of breakdowns, fearful that the pain of facing the truth will be too much to bear. Many choose to remain in the comfort of familiarity rather than confront the reality of their situation. Not knowing, the beginning of a breakthrough is lying inside their mouths on the tongue and it's via the vehicle of spoken words, with first being honest to oneself, "To thine own self be true," Psalm 23:3. We are not able to heal anything that we are not willing to speak.

It does not matter how much we try to live in denial or pretend that everything is fine; there is only one thing that will set us free: the truth. As difficult as it is to face, the truth is one of the keys to healing. This position may seem like one of defeat, but in reality, it's a position of strength and courage. It takes incredible bravery to look at yourself and say, "I'm messed up, and I need help."

You can't escape the truth. Wherever you go, there you are. No matter how far you run or how deeply you hide, the pain, thoughts, memories, hurt, trauma, and attempts to suppress emotions you carry will follow you until you face it. It's easy to spot people who are walking around in denial—just take a look the next time you're in public. You'll see people smiling, going about their daily business, but if you look closer, take the time, and look into the eyes, as the eyes are the gateway to the soul, you sometimes will see that if you are attuned to the spirit, something more is happening. It's almost as if they are "walking dead"—going through the motions while dying on the inside. Their bodies have risen to meet the day, but their spirit and soul are trapped, suffering beneath the weight of unresolved pain. Think about how many people you know or have known who were in the roughest battles of their lives, but when they exited their homes into the public, they put on "the face."

It's a burdensome position to be in, especially when a broken heart is involved. When we are hurting from betrayal, loss, or grief, it feels safer to hide behind the mask of "everything's fine" rather than admit we are messed up. But that kind of denial only adds to the pain. The longer we avoid the truth, the heavier the burden becomes, until one day we find ourselves completely consumed by it. And, if not careful, whether subconsciously, or consciously, hurting and leaving a trail of bodies behind us due to our negligence with mishandling people... which ultimately is another reflection of the dis-ease we have been unable to identify, resulting in this perpetual cycle of pain.

It's important to understand a principle that may sound cliché but is profoundly true and impactful: *"Hurt people hurt people."* Whether consciously or subconsciously, those who are hurting often inflict pain on others, not out of malice, but because they haven't learned how to process or properly handle their own emotions. Unfortunately, others become victims of the residue of that internal pain. This creates yet another layer we must confront, because we all will reap what we sow. We may not reap it in the same form or from the same person, but eventually, the consequences of our actions return to us. As the Word says: *"Be not deceived; God is not mocked: for whatsoever a man soweth, that shall he also reap."* —Galatians 6:7

Without delving into the details of my marital issues, I learned the lesson that love alone cannot sustain a relationship without trust, discipline, and mutual respect. The problem was that I was losing myself in the process. I was allowing someone else's actions to define my worth. I let someone else's choices dictate how I saw myself—unworthy, unloved, and not enough. It took years of betrayals to recognize the truth: my worth was already defined by the Most High and not by another's opinion of me or the mistreatment of me that left me feeling less than.

The Bible teaches us that our value comes from God, not from others' opinions or actions. Psalm 139:14 declares, "I praise you because I am fearfully and wonderfully made; your works are wonderful, I know that full well." This verse reminded me that my identity and value were rooted in God's creation.

I realized that even in my darkest moments, God saw me and valued me. He reminded me that I was not forgotten—and that I was not defined by someone else's choices.

Through this journey, I've learned that healing begins when you stop looking for validation from others and start seeing yourself as God sees you—worthy, loved, and whole. No matter what someone else does, your worth remains intact. You are enough because He says you are.

I had endured so much, but the last straw truly sent me over the edge. I experienced the unthinkable, and it released a part of me I had never experienced before. I was unraveling and on an emotional rollercoaster. There were moments of rage, moments of deep sadness. I acted out in ways I never imagined I would, but through it all, God never left me.

Healing started when I stopped focusing on the heartaches and started focusing on myself. I learned that forgiveness wasn't about excusing mistreatment. It was about releasing the grip that pain had on my life. I had to let go to be free. In other words, I had to relinquish control to gain control of myself.

So, when you find yourself saying, "I'm messed up," remember this: You're not broken, you're in progress. Every scar tells a story, but it doesn't define you. Healing starts when you choose to see yourself as worthy of love, wholeness, honor, and respect, even when others fail to return the same. Healing begins when you admit, "I'm messed up," and allow God to work through your pain to bring you into a place of wholeness.

We can't run from ourselves. No matter how much we try to deny it, there is no escaping the need for healing. So when you admit to yourself that you're hurting, know that you've taken the first step toward freedom. There is strength in saying, "I'm messed up," because it opens the door to the truth. And the truth, no matter how painful it may seem, is what will ultimately set you free.

JOURNAL PROMPT

What experiences have made you feel "messed up"? Write about a time when you let someone else's or your actions shape how you saw yourself. How can you reclaim your worth and start healing today?

captivating

Let the embodiment of
your presence do the
<u>captivating</u>. Before you
speak, who you are, should
have already spoken.

STEPHANIE P. GREEN

Chapter 3

FEAR OF THE UNKNOWN

• • •

"For I know the plans I have for you," declares the Lord, "plans to prosper you and not to harm you, plans to give you hope and a future."

— *Jeremiah 29:11*

Fear has a way of paralyzing us, especially when we're faced with the unknown. I found myself questioning: "What now? What comes next?"

You can remain in toxicity for so long that it begins to feel familiar—even comfortable. I was afraid of the pain, the loneliness, the uncertainty that comes with starting over.

But here's what I learned: fear thrives in the unknown—but growth happens there too. When I finally allowed myself to step into uncertainty, to move beyond the fear, I discovered a strength I didn't know I had.

It's not that I stopped being afraid; I simply stopped letting fear dictate my decisions. I had convinced myself of a lie—a false prediction of a future filled with lack. I told myself I wouldn't survive, that I couldn't make it, that life would be impossible without what I was holding onto. These were all lies I unknowingly came into agreement with.

That's how fear works—it traps you by painting a hopeless picture of the future. And when we believe it, we align ourselves with its deception, allowing it to rob us of hope, joy, and possibility.

But God doesn't promise a life free of hardship—He promises to walk with us through it. I learned to lean into my faith and trust that even when I couldn't see the next step, God was already preparing the path ahead.

That's the thing about the unknown—it's only scary until you step into it.

The fear of leaving, and of letting go, was real. But once I released the life I had clung to so tightly, I made space for something greater. I made space for healing, for joy, for new beginnings... for *me*.

A new awakening.

So, when you feel the fear creeping in, remember this: Fear doesn't get the final say. The unknown is not your enemy—it's your opportunity to evolve, to trust, and to step into the life that is awaiting you.

It can be scary stepping into a place of newness in your life—what many call "the unknown." Life as you once knew it may no longer be the same. It's possible that every person you thought you could depend on is now gone—no longer in your life, unavailable, far away, or even transitioned. You may find yourself in a place with no relatives or friends, as I once did.

There will be days when you have no idea what you're doing. And that's normal.

Be honest and simply say...

- ❧ I don't know what I am doing,
- ❧ I don't know what to do,
- ❧ I don't know what I need to do,
- ❧ I don't know how to make this happen,
- ❧ I don't know how to start,

I will challenge you and say, yes, you do know. The bigger problem may be that you just won't start, due to fear of the unknown. Start. Present something for God to work with on your behalf.

How do I do this? I encourage you to wake up every day and put one foot in front of the other as you devise a plan with the provision of God's help, "For I know the plans I have for you," declares the Lord, "plans to prosper you and not to harm you, plans to give you hope and a future."

— Jeremiah 29:11

Speaking of plans, start to develop a vision for your life. Close your eyes and imagine and think where you want to be, who you want to become, and where to start the process in the direction you desire to go. This process may take some time if you are not accustomed to prayer, visualization, and meditation. "And the LORD answered me, and said, Write the vision, and make it plain upon tables, that he may run that readeth it. For the vision is yet for an appointed time, but at the end it shall speak, and not lie: though it tarry, wait for it; because it will surely come, it will not tarry. "

-Habakkuk 2:2-3

Please don't be in a rush; yet, take your time and see yourself in the future.

Then, take the vision to paper. Write out exactly what you envision—down to the emotions connected to each image. This is not the time to think small or settle for mediocrity. Think as big, as bold, and as expansive as your imagination will allow. Go there.

This is part of your transformation—becoming unrecognizable to your old self—as you begin to trust and believe God to do what you cannot do on your own. If your vision doesn't make you at least a little uncomfortable, chances are it's not big enough. Stretch higher. You are in a season of reestablishing a new you, and with that comes the birth of a new identity.

Once the vision is clear, it's time to set manageable goals to bring it to life. This goal-setting process allows the vision to take root and manifest—what I call *The Awakening*. In this stage, we move from dreaming to doing. We begin to break the vision down into actionable steps that lead to real progress. The key is not to become so overwhelmed that you give up before you begin.

Stephanie, how do you know?

Let me be honest: writing this book is a testament to everything I'm sharing with you. I know I've been called to empower women through this process, yet I stopped writing many times—for countless reasons. And while the reasons felt valid, the truth is, who am I to ignore the calling placed on my life to speak life to my sisters—my aunts, mothers, grandmothers, nieces, cousins, and women across the world?

This is your reminder: when you're stepping into something you've never done before, distractions will come. Obstacles will arise. Excuses will feel justified. But if you're not careful, you'll lean into those negative energies instead of pushing forward. Stay in a forward posture. Complete the assignment given to you.

The world needs the version of you that is yet to be revealed.

Sis, do not expect everything to be easy or go smoothly. In fact, it's often quite the opposite. When opposition comes, that's your cue to *embrace the assignment* and go harder than ever before. Why? Because the plan for your life is shifting—pulling you into a realm you've never walked in before. It's unknown, yes, but it's divinely ordered. And it will require you to trust the process—and even more, to trust the One who gave you the vision.

The vision has now been birthed and broken down into manageable portions. Now it's time to enter the *implementation* stage. This is where you take what has been imparted to you—one goal at a time—and begin the work. Let me remind you: this isn't a Kentucky Derby sprint. This is more like a graceful, intentional stride on a mystic black stallion.

Set target dates to check in with yourself—assess your progress, adjust your steps, and prepare for the next phase... and the next... and the next. You get the point.

> By this time, as you work the process, the fear of the unknown should begin to fade. Because "God has not given us the spirit of fear, but of power, and of love, and of a sound mind."
>
> —2 Timothy 1:7

Too many of us have walked in the unknown with hesitation—living beneath our privileges, shortening the Hand of God through unbelief, and hardening our hearts by accepting the lie that *"this is it."*

But I serve notice today: this is *not* the end. This is just the beginning—your introduction to a new identity.

Remember the three Hebrew boys? They were thrown into a fiery furnace because they refused to bow to idols. In the natural, it looked like death. But in the spirit, it was the doorway to life. The Word says they came out not smelling like smoke, not looking like what they'd been through—unshaken, untouched, and unbound.

Sis, *Get Up.* You're coming out better. You're coming out blessed. You're coming out free, strengthened, powerful, bold, wiser, and favored—with the covering of divine protection over your life.

"It has not yet appeared what you shall become." But know this: what's coming is greater.

I can speak life over you because I am you, and you are me. You are more than a conqueror, and any and everything that is trying or designed to bring you death. I decree and declare life and life more abundantly. Sis, focus your eyes only on what you need to do, do the work that has been placed in your hands to accomplish, and then let God add his super to your innate power because He is just that intrinsic. It is impossible for you to be bestowed with such a mighty vision and be deserted without provision, resources, and connections to bring it to fruition. You are the solution to the problem(s) others need, right now. We must be obedient, intentional, and actively be in pursuit of the vision. You see, the vision is not just about you or me, but it's much bigger than we are. You are the vessel to bring it to life.

Therefore, you don't need another sign, prophecy, or confirmation… you only need to take *ACTION.*

Nevertheless, just in case you do… *this is your sign.*

(**Insert your name here**)—get up, get intentional, and implement what you need to do.

Yes, that thing on the inside of you that won't loose you, that keeps pulling and tugging on your heart—the thing you keep trying to forget, but it keeps coming back up within you. Yes, *that.* Take hold of it. A greater purpose is calling you. *Higher is calling.*

Sis, could it be possible that sometimes we don't see progress because we haven't done what we were told to do the first time? I once heard it said like this: *"The anointing is in the instructions."*

What does that mean? It means the power needed to complete what we are called to do is found in the obedience to act. The ability to bring forth the vision is connected to following the instructions we've already been given. The fulfillment we desire lies in the *"what"* we have yet to come into full agreement with.

I'm reminded of when the Angel of the Lord appeared to Moses in a flame of fire from the midst of a bush that burned but was not consumed. God called out to Moses and told him to remove his shoes, for the ground he was standing on was holy.

God spoke of the affliction of His people in Egypt and declared that He had come to deliver them into a land flowing with milk and honey. He told Moses He was sending him to Pharaoh to demand the release of His people. God even explained what Pharaoh would do, but most importantly, He explained what *He* would do—including the signs and wonders that would follow.

Yet even after God's assurance, Moses was still afraid and raised multiple objections.

Let that be your reminder: even when fear shows up, obedience must rise higher.

Moses raised another objection to GOD: "Master, please, I don't talk well. I've never been good with words, neither before nor after you spoke to me. I stutter and stammer." GOD said, "And who do you think made the human mouth? And who makes some mute, some deaf, some sighted, some blind? Isn't it I, GOD? So, get going. I'll be right there with you—with your mouth! I'll be right there to teach you what to say." He said, "Oh, Master, please! Send somebody else!" GOD got angry with Moses: "Don't you have a brother, Aaron the Levite? He's good with words, I know he is. He speaks very well. In fact, at this very moment, he's on his way to meet you. When he sees you, he's going to be glad. You'll speak to him and tell him what to say. I'll be right there with you as you speak and with him as he speaks, teaching you step by step. He will speak to the people for you. He'll act as your mouth, but you'll decide what comes out of it. Now take this staff in your hand; you'll use it to do the signs." Exodus 4:10-17

The truth of the matter is, IF GOD BE FOR YOU, WHO CAN BE AGAINST YOU? Whatever insecurities, hang-ups, shortcomings, or even perceived deformities we may think we have—it doesn't matter. God can use any of us, exactly as we are right now, for His glory. We simply have to position ourselves and move forward with what He has instructed us to do.

When you're walking in the unknown, don't expect—or seek—perfection. The vision God gave you likely didn't show the failed attempts, sleepless nights, frustration, fear, or detours. But those are all part of the journey. To rise higher, you'll have to go deeper.

Also, don't expect everyone—friends, associates, acquaintances, or even those closest to you—to support or encourage you. This level of newness you're stepping into will require a stretching of your faith.

"Without faith, it is impossible to please God." And when you move in obedience, God will send the right people—those assigned to help bring the vision to life.

In my transformation, I learned from a Man of God, "In the natural world we see with our eyes open, but in the spirit, we see better with our eyes closed."-James D. Edwards, TFCC. This means the necessity to learn how to tap into the spirit to listen to the voice of God for clarity, instructions, guidance, and direction. Our natural eyes can get us in trouble, causing us to feel defeated before we even begin and leading us to miss out on the blessings meant for us. However, when you realize that it is not necessarily based on what you see physically but rather what you know and see in the spirit, and who is guiding you on the journey, the situation immediately shifts in your favor.

JOURNAL PROMPT

What are you most afraid of when it comes to the unknown? Write about a time when fear held you back. How can you step into that unknown today, trusting that something greater is waiting on the other side?

Stop

"Stop overriding your intuition and giving the benefit of the doubt. Sis, sometimes it's the doubt that is alarming you to retreat, take heed and move wiser."

STEPHANIE P. GREEN

Chapter 4

EITHER WAY, IT'S GONNA HURT

• • •

"Weeping may endure for a night,
but joy comes in the morning."

— Psalm 30:5

WHETHER YOU CHOOSE TO STAY IN PAIN OR RISE TO BECOME FREE, IT WILL HURT

Pain is inevitable. That's another one of the grievous lessons to learn and accept. Whether I stayed in the marriage or walked away, processed the unexpected deaths, endured the losses and faced having to start over, I was still going to hurt. Either way, I had to face the reality of my situation: the betrayal, the lies, the broken trust, deaths, losses, starting over etc. There was no path forward that didn't involve pain. But the real question became, "What kind of pain will lead to my healing?" But here's what I learned: Some pain doesn't lead to healing—it just keeps you bound.

In that moment, I was reminded of the comfort and strength God promises to those who are brokenhearted. Psalm 34:18 says, "The Lord is close to the brokenhearted and saves those who are crushed in spirit." This verse reminded me that even in the depths of hardships I was not alone. God's presence was with me, carrying me through the pain and reminding me that His truth would always outshine the darkness.

There is a hurt; then, there is a kind of hurt that makes you question everything you thought you knew about love, loyalty, and even yourself. But even in the midst of that pain, I realized something: I was still standing. I was stronger than I thought. There is another prolific leader, a mentor of mine and so many other Queens by the name of R.C. Blakes, Jr. who says, **"Sometimes you have to let your heart break so your soul can heal."**

I learned that pain can be a teacher if you let it. It shows you your limits, but it also shows you your strength. It teaches you that some things are worth fighting for—and some things aren't when there is no reciprocation. So, yes, it's going to hurt—either way. But you get to choose the kind of hurt that leads to healing and the kind that keeps you in chains. And once you make that choice, you'll find that on the other side of pain is a strength you never knew you had.

Whatever choice you make will determine which path leads to more favorable results. Sis, please choose you this time. You are worthy of better. You deserve to live and see what the future holds for you.

This chapter is powerful because I have provided an opportunity for you to become an author in your own story. I left this chapter open for you to start rewriting your turnaround for your life. Sis, write everything from your spirit and believe it will come to pass. I love you.

LET'S PRAY...

Jesus, I thank You for my Sister who is working on her turnaround in life. She has endured many heartaches, traumas, and disappointments. Today, she has decided to rewrite her path and walk in the newness of life. You said where two or three are gathered in Your Name, You are in the midst. I stand in agreement with my beautiful Sister, believing that the giants-troubles in her life will no longer have control. We turn towards You, trusting that You will make all wrongs right, all crooked places straight, and turn everything meant for harm into a stunning masterpiece.

Thank You Jesus, for it all, as we believe greater things are on the horizon. She shall live to testify of the goodness of Your grace and how You brought her out of a place of despair into the fullness of **joy**.

In Jesus' name, we pray. **Amen.**

WRITE SIS. WRITE ...

Think about a time when you faced two difficult choices. What kind of pain were you willing to endure? How did you make your decision, and what did you learn about yourself through the process?

sprinkle

If seasoning can help things taste better; then a <u>sprinkle</u> of you should leave a residue of a sacred encounter.

STEPHANIE P. GREEN

Chapter 5

FINDING LIGHT IN THE DARKNESS

• • •

"Thy word is a lamp unto my feet,
and a light unto my path."

- Psalms 119: 105

I never imagined that my story would become an example for others. In the thick of it—when I was drowning —I couldn't see how any good could come from my pain. I was too consumed by the grief, the anger, and the sense of loss. But God had a different plan. He was using my story to shape me into something more than just a survivor. He was turning me into an example of what healing looks like.

It's funny, though, because being an example was never something I sought out. I wasn't trying to be strong or brave—I was just trying to survive. But as I started to heal, I realized that others were watching. My family, my friends, even people in the community—they saw my struggle, and they also saw my strength. They saw how I kept going, even when the weight of everything seemed too heavy to bear.

I learned that our lives aren't just for us. They're for everyone who's walking a similar path, everyone who needs to know that it's possible to come out on the other side. I realized that every tear I cried, every hard decision I made, and every step I took toward healing was not just for me. It was for the women who would come after me—the ones who needed to know that healing is possible, even after the deepest wounds.

Becoming an example wasn't about perfection. It was about honesty. I had to be real with myself and with others about my struggles, my presumed failures, and my victories. I had to be willing to show my scars and share the lessons I'd learned. Through this process, I discovered that vulnerability isn't weakness—it's strength. And in that vulnerability, others are able to understand they are not alone.

So, when I say, "You will be the example of healing manifested," I mean, you will be the living proof and reminder that, no matter how deep the pain, there is a way through. People are watching, but more than that, they are learning. You have the power to show them what it looks like to rise after a fall, to heal after heartbreak, and to grow after loss.

Here is a vulnerable moment, because I know what comes from the heart reaches the heart. During the course of writing this book, has everything been great, no; have I done everything right, no; have I made some mistakes, yes; and, have I been hurt, yes. Why is it important for me to elaborate on this point? One of the ways you will be tested regarding your growth, healing, deliverance…will oftentimes be in the same area or closely linked to the past trauma, pain, hurt experienced etc. However, you come through the test will be an indicator of the areas of improvement that are needed and will also indicate the growth and healing that has occurred. I am evidence of an imperfect-perfect woman who is daily striving to walk in purpose, power, and being a source of strength to every woman that is in need of healing.

"I will praise thee; for I am fearfully and wonderfully made: marvellous are thy works; and that my soul knoweth right well." -Psalms 13-14

JOURNAL PROMPT:

Think about a time when you realized others were watching your journey. How did that influence your healing process? In what ways can you be an example of strength and healing to those around you?

protect

<u>Protect</u> your senses - What
you see, hear, touch, taste,
and smell, as energy will
find a source of entry.

Remember, what you allow
to penetrate can dominate.

STEPHANIE P. GREEN

Chapter 6

THE JOURNEY OF HEALING

• • •

"He heals the brokenhearted and binds up their wounds."

— Psalm 147:3

Healing is not linear, it is not a straight line. It's a journey with twists, turns, setbacks, and breakthroughs. For me, the process of healing my wounded soul was nothing short of a battle. There were days when I felt like I was making progress, and then there were days when the heaviness of my heart would pull me right back down. But through it all, I learned that healing isn't about forgetting what happened or pretending it didn't hurt. It's about learning how to live and thrive despite the wounds.

The pain I carried for so long ran deep. It wasn't just the betrayal, unexpected deaths, losses that hurt me—it was the betrayal of my own self. I had abandoned myself in so many ways. That realization was a turning point. I knew that if I wanted to truly heal, I had to start by reclaiming myself.

It wasn't easy. The wounds were raw, and some days it felt like they would never close. But little by little, I started to heal. I found that healing wasn't about patching things up quickly; it was about tending to the wound, giving it time, and allowing myself the grace to feel everything—the anger, the sadness, the loss, and eventually, the peace. Make a mental note of this, healing is a forever journey. I believe one should never stop evolving, elevating, growing in life and in so doing, guess what, there will be triumphs and hardships along the way ultimately requiring a forever quest in continuous healing. The good news is, our past experiences would have built our stamina to overcome more gracefully if we made the decision to face our giants.

I had to stop looking for other people to speak life over me, and I had to stop expecting closure from those who hurt me. True healing began when I decided to forgive—not for them, but for me. Forgiveness didn't mean excusing the behavior or allowing it to continue. It meant releasing the hold that the pain had over my heart.

Through the process, I rediscovered my worth. I realized that my value wasn't tied to how others treated me or whether or not they recognized their wrongs. I found that healing is about reclaiming your power, your joy, and your peace. It's about filling the empty spaces within yourself with peace, love, and light, instead of seeking it from someone else to do it. It teaches you when you discover any person, place or thing that is not aligned with you to gracefully dismiss yourself as swiftly as possible. God's sovereign power is so incredible, sometimes when you are praying asking for protection etc. you may not have to dismiss yourself because the person, place, or thing will actually dismiss you. And, it is not rejection, discardment, or denial, it's actually protection and redirection for your highest good. Stand in gratitude knowing there is no good thing that God will withhold from you. "For the Lord God is a sun and shield: the Lord will give grace and glory: no good thing will he withhold from them that walk uprightly." -Psalms 84:11

Yes, my soul was wounded, but it wasn't destroyed. And neither is yours. Healing is a process—a slow, intentional, and sacred process. But it is possible. With every step I took towards healing, I became stronger, more whole, and more connected to the person I was always meant to be.

JOURNAL PROMPT:

What wounds are you still carrying? Write about one area of your life where you need healing. How can you begin the process of tending to that wound today?

allow

"You allow what you
believe to be true no
matter how dysfunctional
it may be."

STEPHANIE P. GREEN

Chapter 7

LEVELING UP

• • •

"But they that wait upon the Lord shall renew their strength; they shall mount up with wings as eagles; they shall run, and not be weary; and they shall walk, and not faint."

-Isaiah 40-31

At some point, survival isn't enough. There comes a time when you realize that you don't just want to heal—you want to thrive. That's when I knew it was time to level up.

Leveling up wasn't about proving anything to anyone else. It was about reclaiming my life on my terms. After years of giving and sacrificing, I knew it was time to invest in me. I wasn't just a survivor of my circumstances.

It wasn't an easy transition. There's a level of comfort in staying in the familiar, even when that comfort comes from toxicity. It's important that we take ownership of any dysfunctionality in our doings and engagements too. There is no way toxicity can thrive in of itself.

Leveling up required me to let go of old beliefs and habits that kept me stuck in a place of complacency. It meant acknowledging that I deserved better—better love, better opportunities, better for myself. That realization was both freeing and terrifying.

One of the first steps I took toward leveling up was setting boundaries. For the first time in my life, I started saying "no" to things that didn't serve me. I no longer allowed people to have access to me if they couldn't honor my worth. I learned that boundaries aren't locks to keep people out—they're doors that protect the peace you've fought so hard to find. And it was through those boundaries that I started to see myself differently.

I also began investing in my growth. I sought out therapy, surrounded myself with positive influences, and started focusing on the things that brought me joy. Leveling up was about more than just external changes—it was about the internal work. I became intentional about my healing, my self-care, and my spiritual growth. I wasn't just getting by anymore—I was soaring.

Leveling up meant walking in purpose. I began to understand that my story had value, not just for me but for others. My pain had a purpose, and that purpose was to show others that they, too, can rise. I started to see the possibilities in my life again—the dreams that had been buried were now resurfacing, and I was ready to live them.

This is what I want you to understand: leveling up is not just about moving on—it's about moving forward with clarity and intentionality. It's about choosing yourself, about recognizing that you are worthy of the best that life has to offer, and then going after it. It's about stepping into the fullness of who you are meant to be, without apology.

HERE ARE 10 WAYS TO, GET UP.

Ways to Get Up:

1. **Ask God:** "God, this is not a good situation, and I need You to deliver me and make me free from [insert your burden]."

2. **Believe:** Trust that once you have asked God for His help in freeing you, it is done. You will need to make an intentional choice to give whatever "IT" may be to Him.

3. **Forgive:** Forgiveness is not a choice but a necessity to move into the blessings that await you. Unforgiveness will choke the breath out of anything fruitful that tries to enter your life. If you want to see a shift in your circumstances, it's mandatory to forgive so you can collect the harvest in your season.

4. **Live:** Life may look a lot different now. This is the perfect opportunity to redefine who you are. Understand who you are, what your purpose is, what vision/legacy you want to leave for your children/family, and how you see your new life. Set boundaries, establish standards, and embrace this new season.

5. **Embrace the Shift:** What is a shift? A shift is when something is moved, turned, or changed. You have been shifted into a new position and direction to birth a new you. The surrendering process is required to dispose of old patterns and habits and bring forth a life you never knew before. The process of becoming who you are meant to be is contingent upon your willingness to go willingly or involuntarily. Here's the caveat: either way, you are going, so you may as well choose to go willingly.

6. **Mindset:** The way you interpret your change will heavily influence the trajectory of your future. Your mindset will either cause you to rise higher or bring you beneath your God-given privileges. You decide how to embrace what may seem like defeat, trauma, or a negative experience. Wherever your mind goes, your body will follow.

7. **Prayer:** Prayer is the key that opens the spiritual realm for us to share our admiration, worship, praise, and communicate with God concerning the matters of the heart. I encourage you to tap into the Holy Spirit and pray in your heavenly language. Develop a relationship with God, as the scripture says, "Though we know not how to pray as we ought, the Spirit gives utterance."

8. **GET UP:** No one is coming to save you. **YOU** will have to GET UP and walk in the power and authority provided to you, knowing there is a greater purpose ahead of you than the dark pit you experienced or may be currently experiencing. To not GET UP is to say that you have accepted defeat and succumbed to the lie that this is as good as it gets. That's a lie. The only truth to that lie is that it will be true if you choose to quit.

9. **Heal:** Healing hurts. You must heal as a whole person—single, complete. In other words, become one with yourself. Discover you. Learn how to be fulfilled and comfortable being with yourself. Focus on developing a new identity, create business plans, and work on becoming healthier. Please understand that time doesn't heal anything; **healing** heals as you heal.

10. **Watch Your Mouth:** One of the strongest muscles in your body is the tongue. It has the power to speak blessings or curses. When you speak, the words that exit your mouth are on an energy frequency that will create either life or death. You have the power to choose whether you will live or die by what you speak. Choose life—you deserve it.

BONUS:

11. **Understand the Nature of Pain:** Whether caused by heartbreak, betrayal, deaths, abuse or something else, pain will bring mood shifts, anger, grief, disbelief, suffering, and more. "Be ye angry, but sin not." We are human, touched by the infirmities of this world

and others. This is a natural response to situations that have caused pain. Don't think it's strange when these emotions arise. They could be indicators that more healing is needed or warnings to protect you from future harm.

12. **Navigation System:** It may be necessary to connect with a trusted source who can help you navigate through this time. This could include the Word of God, a psychotherapist, spiritual counseling, a support group, or a grounded spiritual coach/leader. I would strongly recommend to know whomever that labor amongst you. Everyone with a "title" is not assigned to you. Seek His face for direction.

13. **Resist Revenge:** "Vengeance is Mine," says the Lord. DO NOT SEEK TO GET EVEN. What we do to others we will reap which means it's already done to us. We cannot hurt someone else without first hurting ourselves. Why lower yourself to their level? The best revenge is to keep illuminating, evolving, and elevating. "Greater is He that is in you than he that is in the world." 1 John 4:4

14. **Isolation:** There may be many days and nights when you may be alone and feel lonely. Be mindful to not allow the emotional state of loneliness to direct your thoughts to do so will be detrimental to your growth as the desire for companionship can be strong during this time. In order to elevate, separation and isolation is certain to visit you. These feelings are normal and congruent with the journey you are on.

15. **Do Not Make Major Decisions:** This is the time to stand still and wait for instructions. Be patient and seek God's guidance. This way decisions will not be made based on your emotions but grounded in truth and life.

16. **Focus on Yourself:** Become so immersed and intentional in improving every area of your life that you transform into the best version of yourself.

17. **Progression:** Please do not measure yourself or progression based on the journey of someone's else's life remember they too have unspoken hurdles.

18. **Look in the Mirror:** Take inventory of yourself. There are questions that one should ask such as: why did **(I)** allow…, why did **(I)** stay…, how did **(I)** get in such a position, why did **(I)** give my power away, etc. Oftentimes, the person we should be most disappointed in is looking back at us. Sis, sometimes it's not <u>them</u>, it's <u>you</u>. I know that may be challenging to hear; yet; necessary for deliverance. Did you lack self confidence? Do you feel afraid to exit? Did you not understand your worth and value? Is it the lie we tell ourselves based on the (child)ren? The reasons can be astronomical. And, until we accept full accountability and responsibility for our actions or the lack thereof we will be unable to fully be able to embrace the new journey which is prepared before us.

19. **Read #1 Again:** You can't stop—you have to keep moving. ARISE, you have the power within to overcome.

YOU CAN NOT STOP, YOU'VE GOT TO KEEP ELEVATING AND RISE HIGHER, AS YOU HAVE THE POWER—USE IT TO COME THROUGH. I'M PRAYING WITH YOU!

JOURNAL PROMPT:

What does leveling up look like for you? In what areas of your life do you need to set new boundaries or invest in your growth? Write about how you can take the next step toward thriving in your purpose.

embrace

Embrace the power within you that you may be able to see the reflection of the power source sustaining you.

STEPHANIE P. GREEN

Chapter 8

AWAKENING THE QUEEN WITHIN

• • •

"You are altogether beautiful, my darling;
There is no flaw in you."

— Song of Solomon 4:7

The reflection of who you are inwardly will automatically shine brightly outwardly. There is a Queen on the inside of us that desperately wants to rise hence the importance of healing.

As we move towards the discovery of this new woman we have and/ or are becoming there is a mandate to never live beneath who we are created to be. There must be a level of assurance and confidence flowing within that anything or anyone that remotely threatens to bring you down from evolving immediately must be removed. One of the ways we can do this is understanding who we are, and whose we are and having a spirit of discernment, and LEAVING or removing yourself immediately when you are no longer being appropriately honored or respected.

There is a certain way Queen's move. There is a silent, resilient, confidence and knowing within when you know who you are. Queens can walk in any room and not be intimidated as she understands: There is no one greater than me, there is no one beneath me, but I am equal to all. (Bishop RC Blakes, Jr.). A Queen understands she has the power to shift any environment she's placed in because the energy she walks in is transformative. Be mindful once you start to embrace this power there will be people that are subject not to welcome you for no reason and some will be intrigued wanting to know "what is it about you." Either way, that is not your concern.

It is a fact that Queens embrace and celebrate other Queens. When you see your Sister doing great from one sister to another we celebrate and uplift them. This is what a sisterhood really is, we can get done more together unified as one than being divisive. When necessary, I encourage you to seek your tribe, introduce yourself to others when you are out, place yourself around like-minded women and make sure to properly vet them. I often move alone as I have embodied the power of self.

Queens embody an essence that others are unable to explain but certainly can feel. You may hear statements such as: "There's something about you; you got It; where did you come from; you are powerful; you make me feel ___; you are different..." And, yes, you will get stares and at first may make you uncomfortable but eventually you will get used to it as it has nothing to do with what you are "doing" but rather everything you are "being."

Queens learn to take all of their experiences from the most grievous to the joyous ones and everything in between and build upon them for the enrichment of themselves, those around them and the overall community.

The birthing of the book came from painful, grievous experiences to the point I literally thought I would die. You see, though; I was blindsided in more ways than one, from habitual adultery, suffered unexpected deaths, experienced major losses, led me to this very moment where I can speak with power and authority and tell you, SIS, GET UP! You can make it and not only can you make it, you are able to thrive. Now, I am able to be grateful for it all. The hardships suffered pushed me into purpose. I didn't ask for any of this, I didn't pray for it, I wasn't seeking it or anything of its kind. My life shifted in a different direction that I never ever would have imagined had those things never happened.

The anointing comes at a price and we are not afforded the opportunity to input what we think the cost should be. However, we are responsible for when life happens to decide how we respond. I had to wait until Jesus started working on healing me before I strive to reach your heart because as aforementioned: hurt people really do hurt people. I refused to speak venom and bitterness but rather fill my mouth with blessings and that is what I speak over your life. I don't know what you have experienced, may be experiencing, or will experience and it is irrelevant for me to know. With that said, Sis, I am here to tell you there is a power source on the inside of you that you can activate right now, this very moment, wherever you are in the world to change the course of your life.

Say this short prayer with me,

Father God, In the Name of Jesus. I first thank you for allowing me to withstand every trial and tribulation I have had to endure to date. I thank you for how you have covered and watched over me even when I didn't know what to ask or seek you for. Jesus, I don't have all the answers but I pray you will lead and guide me to the way of truth, knowledge, and understanding. Impart in me the wisdom needed to execute the plan and vision you have for my life. You said, "You know the plans you have for me, plans to prosper me and not harm me, plans to give me hope and an expected end." Therefore, I am trusting you God to bring restoration, healing, and everything else I am unaware that I need to pray for. God allow me to see your glory and hand in my life. Thank you for your covering. And, I thank you in advance for answering my prayers. I decree and declare that I shall become all you have purposed for me to become in this life.

In Jesus Name. Amen.

This prayer is to get you started. You can add to it; however, you desire. And, frankly if all the word(s) you have to say is, Jesus. Then, that is a prayer in itself.

Sis, you already have the victory but you are required, mandated, to GET UP and start walking. Tears may flow down your face, pain may compass your heart, fear may try to overcome you but you must push through. There were many nights and days I was laid prostrate before God. He does not respond to tears but He does respond to His Word.

Speak the Word of God out of your mouth. How do I do this? For example, if you are struggling with fear. Go find the scriptures that addresses fear "Fear thou not; for I am with thee: be not dismayed; for I am thy God: I will strengthen thee; yea, I will help thee; yea, I will uphold thee with the right hand of my righteousness." -Isa 41:10. Pray and meditate on this scripture and trust the Word that is spoken until it becomes alive in you.

The hardships endured will develop the better and greater version of you if you choose for it to do so. When God does release/deliver you, do go seek forgiveness and be released if you haven't already done so.

Forgiveness is an absolute requirement for the elevation of your life. No, the memories, hurt, emotions, etc. will not disappear as this is what healing is designed for. But, God will give you PEACE in the midst of the transformation. Every time the thought or memory tries to invade your mind in an attempt to bring you down, speak the Word of God over it. You must learn how to fight spiritually as you have been in spiritual warfare. "For the weapons of our warfare are not carnal, but mighty through God to the pulling down of strong holds;" 2 Corinthians 10:4.

Sis, let's be honest: if it were up to us, we'd never choose to endure pain or suffering. We cling to the illusion of control, but life has a way of humbling us, turning us in every direction until we have no choice but to let go.

Yet, even in the chaos, we are never without refuge. As Psalm 91:1 reminds us, "Whoever dwells in the shelter of the Most High will rest in the shadow of the Almighty." Wherever life takes us, we are equipped with God's grace, His power, and His promise of protection. No matter how far we fall or how hard the journey becomes, we can rise and overcome through the power that works within us.

There is no greater gift we can provide ourselves than healing. Knowing who we are, whose we are, walking in confidence, and being purposeful on purpose.

access

Do not be easily accessible.

<u>Access</u> to you should be a
rarity not a normalcy.

STEPHANIE P. GREEN

Here are several pointers to keep in mind as you establish Queen-ship:

1. Develop a stronger intimate relationship with Christ Jesus.

2. Learn how to take a compliment by saying a simple, Thank you.

3. Denounce the "You Strong" and/or "I'm a Strong Woman" statement. I am a witness that "strong" people don't receive help. The perception is, "they're good, they're fine, they're okay," which at times couldn't be farther from the truth. The fact is, we that are placed in such positions, have no other choice but to be "resilient." I understand most who make such statements don't mean anything negative rather just don't understand we are human too. Yes, we need and want help but it's rarely if at all given.

4. Get comfortable receiving help when offered. This has been a challenge for me and I am sure for so many others as well. When you have been "IT" for so long and not had anyone else to turn towards; you have to make things happen no matter what it takes. We just figure it out on our own. Become comfortable receiving help when offered no matter the form it may come in i.e taking groceries to the car, lifting a heavy box, etc.

5. Learn the difference between Intentional vs. Attention. Intentional is when there is purpose, vision, plan, consistency, goals... while giving attention is momentarily time and space often given when it's convenient for the other individual.

6. You are worthy and deserving of honor, respect, and love first from yourself and then by anyone you allow to enter your life. Anything or anybody that disrupts your peace costs too much and will need to be removed expeditiously.

7. Get out your head and stop talking yourself out of blessings. When a decision is made, stay the course of the plan. There are 100 million, What If's?...

8. Know the difference between "lonely" versus "being alone". Sis, please don't let being lonely make you make irrational decisions that you would never normally make if you were not. This stage can be critical as it potentiallly can alter the path of acceleration you are working towards and have you turning backwards instead of moving forward.

9. TAKE YOUR TIME. Slow down and stop giving too much too soon. TIME coupled with actions and consistency will be the decipher in whether someone is really for you or not. Those that leave were going to leave anyway once they got whatever they wanted from you.

10. Stop (Do)ing and start (Be)coming-(Be)ing.

11. Become every quality you want in another individual. Do not seek or ask someone for anything that you are not. I have learned that many expect others to provide for them the things they do not possess for themselves ie. I just want peace...Are you peaceful? I just want to be happy. Are you happy? Most of what is desired by others are internal qualities that only can be intrinsically manifested from within ourselves and not by anyone else. I can add to your peace, but I can not be your peace. Anyone that enters your life should be an addition to the peace, happiness etc. you already possess. This is what it means by complimenting each other well.

12. Protect your senses (sight smell, touch, sound, and taste). The senses are another pathway to our soul. I encourage you to be mindful of how and what you allow to penetrate your senses.

13. Adopt a renewed mindset. It is no longer "what if" followed by negative commentary but rather: I can, I will, I shall...

14. There will be times when you may become exhausted, frustrated, feeling like you are not making progress, don't know how things will change, lost, alone, unsupported, concerned about your future and

the list goes on. During these times you will need to remind your-selves that feelings are fleeting and can get you in trouble. There are times when it's not about how you necessarily feel but rather what you know to be true. What is true? The truth is, you are more than a conqueror and you will GET UP again, and again, and again.

15. You don't have to force anything that is ready.

16. Learn how to shift the room when you enter and capture the essence of other's energy when they encounter you. Everybody should leave better after experiencing you. Literally.

17. Invest in yourself. Believe in you. Bet on you.

18. Move in silence. Learn how to execute in the darkness to the point you don't have to shine the light because the evidence will be unde-niable that it will break through on its own.

19. Queens don't ask for permission, we walk in authority and manifest by placing our hands to work toward the vision at hand.

20. Never let anybody tell you more than once they don't want you. And, you don't have to wait until the words are verbally expressed. It's not all about what they say, it's what they do. You hear what they say, and you watch what they do too. Then, you move accordingly.

21. You are not a yo-yo or spin top when they try to return… return them back to the sender. You must maintain standards and re-member why they are no longer in your life. The only exception to this rule may be: ONLY if you see transformation, consistency, intentional change, should you ever consider allowing someone you deemed worthy to return into your life. Please do not EVER allow a return without consulting God first.

22. Do not choose anyone who does not choose you and/or has chosen someone over you.

23. Become relentless in your pursuit to wholeness.

24. "You will be led by what you're full of…" (read that again) bitterness, pain, hatred will bleed through the soul and display a depiction contrary to your purpose. Rather, fill yourself with peace, love, light, legacy, etc.

25. You don't need closure. There actions spoke loud enough. Closure is not needed from another individual. Your closure is that, (IT); whatever (IT) is, happened. Don't torture yourself trying to figure out what happened, why…let (IT) go. You have purpose to fulfill. "Stop expecting the person that hurt you, to heal you,"-R.C. Blakes, Jr.

26. People are only able to experience you to the depth in which you are. Sometimes we may not be as grand as we believe ourselves to be. Keep evolving.

27. Whole and healed individuals will not spend too much time trying to knock down walls you have built in an attempt to protect yourself. Their capacity to love you properly will not come at the expense of them losing themselves in the process. They will at some point walk away. Therefore, know when someone has entered your life to elevate you versus to manipulate or cause harm.

28. When there is no clarity, there will be confusion, and where there is confusion, hurt is soon to erupt. Do not manufacture your own pain. Sis, you see the signs; most importantly, your spirit of discernment is not lying…trust it and move accordingly.

29. Do not try to give someone something they already don't want. Let. Them. Go.

30. You are One of One….

31. Priority versus Option. If you are not the Priority, then being someone's Option is not an option. Let's be real, we all have options. The delusion happens when they think, "I will miss out on something

better." There is a sense of confidence that because I have attracted this great person(you) then what else better can I get? It's called a TRAP (self-sabotage). The truth is, you/they may have options but what is the <u>QUALITY</u> and substance of those options is the question. When you know the caliber and quality of woman you are, do not ever become anyone's option.

32. "Giver's have no boundaries; and, Taker's have no limits," when I heard this statement it resonated loudly. Establish your boundaries and hold true to them.

33. "Stop losing sleep over someone that is getting rest with somebody else." Refocus your attention because you have things to accomplish.

34. Tell the TRUTH. Be authentic unapologetically you. Yet, don't become complacent and stop growing. We never "arrive" there will forever be room for continued growth.

35. Please do not hide behind your prayers, meditation, therapy, business(es), and not actively engage in the work to confront past traumas, hurts, disappointments, heartbreaks. What is not addressed will ultimately suppress you. If you ever wonder why continuous cycles are being repeated in your life, check your emotional blockages.

36. "Let people be people." I would have never treated them like that... I desire... but they don't want..." Don't expect a YOU out of them. Learn how to gracefully pivot when you do not align. I promise this will save you from future heartache.

37. GET OUT OF YOUR HEAD AND GET INTO YOUR HEART. Because, out of the abundance of the heart the mouth speaketh. Matt. 12:34. We can not heal anything we are unable to speak. And, we will not allow anyone that was <u>sent to us</u> to come close and to be a blessing being stuck in our head. Keyword: **Sent.** You will know the difference as their spirit will be completely different from anyone you have encountered.

38. NEVER try to convince anyone of your value or worth. If they are unable to identify it there is nothing you will ever be able to say or do to prove it. Your embodiment and essence of the divine can only be appreciated by those who have also evolved as an individual as your reflection will be a mirror to them.

39. We should be striving to maintain our virtue and/or staying abstinent or remain celibate until marriage. Developing unnecessary soul ties and trying to break from them is a process in itself.

40. Read #1 again.

Remember the blessings of the Lord are, Yes and Amen and he added no sorrow to them. Anything forced is not ready. "For all the promises of God in Him are Yes, and in Him Amen, to the glory of God through us." -2 Corinthians 1:20.

There comes a time in every woman's life when she realizes her own power. For me, that moment came when I stopped looking outward for validation and started looking inward. The queen within me had been waiting all along—waiting for me to acknowledge her, to call her forward, and to step into the authority I was always meant to embrace. It wasn't about becoming someone new, but about awakening the strength, grace, and authority that were already inside of me.

For years, I had let others' opinions define who I was. I sought approval from those who couldn't see my worth. I allowed my identity to be shaped by the roles I engaged—wife, mother, friend, business owner—without recognizing that I was so much more. But the journey I went through— led to one undeniable truth: I am a Queen, and it was time I started to embrace it. My name, Stephanie, means Crown. This AWAKENING has changed me.

Awakening the queen within didn't happen overnight. It was a process of unlearning all the ways I had been taught to shrink myself. It meant letting go of the guilt and shame that kept me small. I had to give myself permission to take up space, to be bold, and to step into my purpose without hesitation.

The first step in this awakening was accepting that I am enough, just as I am. I no longer needed to seek love and validation from those who couldn't give it to me. I realized that my value didn't come from others, but from who I am at my core. I am worthy, simply because I exist and HE says, I am made in his image and likeness.

But being a queen also meant taking responsibility for my own happiness. There was no-one who was coming to rescue me or could make me feel complete. I became the hero of my own story. I learned to love myself deeply and unapologetically. I am the definition of a romantic, I love everything about love because that is what I operate within. And as I did, something beautiful happened—I began to attract people and opportunities that aligned with my true self.

Awakening the queen within was about claiming my power, my voice, and my right to live a life that is authentically mine. I started making decisions from a place of confidence and self-love. I set higher standards for myself and my relationships, knowing that I deserved nothing less than the best. I became more intentional about the energy I allowed into my life, surrounding myself with people who uplifted and supported me. I now walk with the confidence of a woman who knows her worth. I speak with the authority of someone who has been through the sufferings and came out stronger. The queen within me has been awakened. Even now, I pray I am uplifting you.

There is a common thread that is spoken which is, anytime God is not the foundation in our lives and we start to place people or anything besides Him in positions they do not belong this will be a sure recipe for destruction. I realize because I put confidence in man was my first mistake, "It is better to trust in the Lord, than to put confidence in man." -Psalm 118:8. What the scripture is saying, man will fail us. And, secondly, when you don't know who you are, and whose you are, then one can easily fall victim to abuse. You have to learn how to stand in authority and cast down everything that does not align with your purpose even if it hurts.

JOURNAL PROMPT:

What does awakening the queen within you look like? Write about a time when you doubted your worth and how you can begin to reclaim your power and walk in your true identity today.

posture

Your name will precede you, which is an extension of your character. Maintain a pure <u>heart posture</u> , and positive motives.

STEPHANIE P. GREEN

Chapter 9

THE POWER OF HEART POSTURE

• • •

SCRIPTURE

"Above all else, guard your heart,
for everything you do flows from it."

— Proverbs 4:23 (NIV)

As we come to the end of this journey, I want to leave you with one final thought, one that holds the key to your continued healing and growth: **heart posture**. In the context of mental health and emotional well-being, heart posture refers to the attitude or inner state of your heart. It encompasses how open, vulnerable, and receptive you are to processing your emotions, connecting with others, and engaging in your healing journey.

Many of us walk through life with guarded hearts, either because we've been hurt in the past or because we fear being vulnerable. But what I've learned, and what I want you to take away, is that healing is impossible without an open heart. Our heart posture plays a crucial role in how we handle pain, connect with others, and move forward in life. We have to get out of our heads and get into our hearts.

The very thing we may be longing for, praying and asking God to answer, when it shows up sometimes many do not know how to receive not to mention handle properly.

Below, I am going to share some pointers for having a healthy heart posture. Be mindful, everybody should not have access to you and particularly not in these vulnerable positions. Please make sure you're opening up to someone who is safe, will know how to handle your heart properly, and the totality of who you are as a whole. Therefore, it is your responsibility to properly vet those you allow to become close to you. If there is any uncertainty, unease, or drawback feelings this is an indicator that you may not be safe with the individual(s) and need to keep it surface level.

With that being said, make sure the uncertainty, uneasiness, etc. is not coming from a <u>place of fear</u>. There are some individuals who are sent into your life to help you heal and navigate through this course of life that you have yet to travel. Receive them in love. A nugget of wisdom is: I would try the spirit by the spirit. What does that mean? Do they align with God; where is the source and foundation of their words rooted within; and are they a reflection of Him, to name a few.

Emotional Openness is the first step toward heart posturing. It's about having the courage to face your emotions, no matter how painful they may be. When your heart is open, you allow yourself to feel and process past trauma, rather than shutting it out. Avoiding your feelings only leads to emotional distress that lingers, manifesting in ways that continue to disrupt your life. By embracing your emotions, you begin to break the cycle and allow yourself to heal.

Vulnerability is often seen as a weakness, but in reality, it too is another great strength you can have. When you are vulnerable, you allow yourself to be seen—by yourself and by others—in your truest form. This openness is the foundation for building meaningful, supportive relationships. It's through these connections that real healing happens, because you no longer carry your burdens alone. Vulnerability invites others into your healing process, and that shared space creates profound growth.

Having a **receptive heart posture** means being willing to heal. It sounds simple, but many of us resist healing because it requires us to change, address emotional blockages, to let go of the pain we've held onto for so long. A heart that is open to healing is ready to embrace growth, to adopt new perspectives, and to accept support from others. It's about being willing to release the things that no longer serve you and to step into the life you truly deserve.

Self-compassion is the one of the greatest gifts you can give yourself. When your heart is compassionate toward yourself, you offer yourself forgiveness, grace, and understanding. Pain often brings guilt, shame, or self-blame, but a heart filled with compassion silences those lies. Instead, it nurtures you through the process, reminding you that you are worthy of healing, that you are enough, just as you are.

Your **heart posture also shapes your connection with others.** If your heart is closed off, it creates distance in relationships. It can make you feel isolated and unsupported, even when you're surrounded by people. It is also subject to make you run especially when you feel that you are getting emotionally close with someone because chances are you quite have never felt the way you do around them with anyone else. But when your heart is open and empathetic, you create authentic connections. These connections are not just important—they are vital. They offer you a lifeline in moments of despair, reminding you that you are not alone on this journey. It is unfair to others to feel like they have to break down walls just to get you to become open. This is a clear indication there are unresolved issues. Ultimately, which can lead to said individuals exiting your life. Heal individuals protect their peace and understand they are unable to give or provide a person with something they do not want and/or unwilling or ready to receive.

Finally, **spiritual alignment** plays a role in heart posture for many. Whether through prayer, meditation, or simply connecting to a higher purpose, having a heart aligned with your spiritual beliefs fosters resilience and peace. It helps you find strength in your darkest moments and offers you a sense of grounding as you navigate the complexities of healing.

In summary, your heart posture is about more than just your emotions. It is a reflection of your openness, your compassion, and your willingness to be vulnerable. It shapes how you process pain, how you connect with others, how you handle others and how you experience healing in mental, emotional, and spiritual ways.

Sis, Get Up—not just with your body, but with your heart. Get up with the openness to heal, with the vulnerability to ask for help, with the compassion to forgive yourself, and with the strength to connect deeply with others. Your heart posture will determine the depth of your healing, and I know, beyond any doubt, that you are capable of rising into the fullness of who you are meant to be.

JOURNAL PROMPT:

Take a moment to reflect on your current heart posture. Are you open to healing, or do you find yourself guarded and closed off? Write about any areas of your life where you need to be more vulnerable, more compassionate with yourself, or more open to receiving support from others. How can you begin to shift your heart posture today?

As you color this page, reflect on the powerful qualities of openness, compassion, vulnerability, and healing. Just as the heart radiates light, let your heart remain open to growth and connection. Coloring each swirl, flower, and beam of light, imagine filling your heart with grace for yourself and others. Embrace vulnerability, knowing it leads to deeper healing and strength.

pain

"Some pain doesn't speak —it settles in the bones, echoes in the silence, and teaches in the stillness."

STEPHANIE P. GREEN

Chapter 10

THE UNSPOKEN WHAT WORDS ARE UNABLE TO CONVEY.

• • •

| SCRIPTURE

"In the same way, the Spirit helps us in our weakness. We do not know what we ought to pray for, but the Spirit himself intercedes for us through wordless groans."

— Romans 8:26

Mental Health:

Mental Health and Physical Health are aligned as it relates to the complexities of taking care of the totality of one's self. The misconception is, mental health has been demoralized as this inhumane, catastrophic negative perception. Would you be surprised if I told you that unattended trauma, stress, depression, etc. will show up in physical symptoms in the body leading to major health conditions and mental breakdowns. In essence the therapy we should be embracing is often disregarded. Sis, this chapter in your life please don't allow anyone to keep you from getting what you need and deserve for your healing. Wherever the mind goes, the body will follow.

There is a hurt, then there is a hurt that words are not able to capture the agony of one's pain. I am a woman who spent 18 years in a marriage and the majority of my youth with a man that after 4 months of the divorce decree was remarried without any notice. The pastor who we went to for marital counseling was the same pastor who remarried him to her armour bearer. The betrayal was beneath disgraceful with all parties. Remember this, don't ever expect betrayal to come from an enemy. Why? Because, from an enemy you should not ever expect anything of substance to be produced. Betrayal will always come from someone you know and least expect to harm you. Betrayal is unexpected, vicious, and blindsides you.

I was then left trying to explain to our son who cried himself to sleep every night that his father was never returning home. I am also a woman who endured the woman who reared and meant everything to me from birth transitioned unexpectedly in her sleep just after speaking to her the night before. Then, only five months later found out my brother was murdered whose body was found in the mountains. And, many other unmentioned hardships which transpired simultaneously all in less than a year.

To say I struggled with my Mental Health is an understatement. The emotional, mental, spiritual and physical turmoil felt like unto death. The sleepless nights, depression, inability to work, clueless what to do next not knowing what and/or if survival was even possible was a recurrent theme that attacked my mind.

Mental Health involves far more than the mind but it impacts every area of a human- being's life to include: mind, body, and soul. Sis, I don't know where you are in life but please understand that if you can lift up your heart to heaven and cry out to Jesus you can make it. Beware you may find yourself in solitude which may result in feelings of loneliness and defeat. Whatever you do, try not to stay in these emotions too long. Though, the emotions are extremely real so honor and respect them. Also, while knowing you are an overcomer, believe the hardship is temporary…you are being refined, purged, and strengthened for the journey. There is a purpose for the pain that will be revealed in due season.

Don't let anyone persuade you that receiving help is not necessary whether this is via therapy, mentorship, coaching etc. Please understand no matter how strong your spiritual foundation is, you can love Jesus and also get therapy too. I found myself not wanting to open myself to love or anyone due to being afraid they would mishandle me. Then, I had to realize, Stephanie, you are pretty dope, have a pure heart posture, Woman of the Most High, the epitome of peace, love, and light. And, I am just a lover's girl/woman. I love everything about love. I have no clue what my future holds but I am now open for blessings to locate me. One of my favorite scriptures puts it like this: "Yes indeed, it won't be long now." God's Decree.

"Things are going to happen so fast your head will swim, one thing fast on the heels of the other. You won't be able to keep up. Everything will be happening at once—and everywhere you look, blessings! Blessings like wine pouring off the mountains and hills. I'll make everything right again for my people Israel: (Amos 9:13 MSG)"

Listen, seasons in life change; therefore, whatever state we find ourselves in we must trust and believe there is purpose. We never know what this life is going to send us but we do know who is in control. And, whatever area in our life we worry the most identifies where we trust God the least. Our life was predestined before birth and we can trust that, "Being confident of this very thing, that he which hath begun a good work in you will perform it until the day of Jesus Christ: Phil 1:6.KJV"

This book was never meant to be a manual—it's a mirror. A reflection of everything you've survived, endured, conquered, and are still rising from. *Sis, Get Up* is not just a phrase, it's a spiritual alarm clock for the soul. It is the nudge that reminds you that there is absolutely life after the breaking, light after the loss, and purpose waiting on the other side of pain. These pages carry the glint of shattered moments—fragments of my truth that, when held to the light, may reflect the broken glass of your own story too. You are not alone. We all can attest to the fact that hurt people do indeed hurt people, but perpetuating brokenness is a choice, and Sis, it's time to choose YOU, choose to be wiser, stronger, and more whole than the pain that tried to break you. It is in fact a choice to be more radiant than the ruins you rose from and more grounded in grace than shaken by grief.

When I reflect on my 'why' for writing this book it was not to glorify the suffering, but to honor the strength it produced. If healing had a language, it would speak like this: painful, raw, yet full of grace. The mission of this book is simple—to give you permission. Permission to feel. To be soft. To break down and rebuild. To stand tall after crawling through grief. To seek therapy. To trust your voice. And most of all, to forgive yourself for what you didn't know then that you now understand. Healing is like a mystery and multi-layered. The way to the treasure (wholeness) is to embrace the journey.

This is your soul's permission slip to live fully again. To love again. To hope wildly again. To rise not as the woman who was burned beyond healing, but as the woman who was *reborn* in her ashes. Everything that tried to destroy you was unknowingly fertilizing the soil of your next season. And guess what? You're about to bloom in a way that silences every doubt and redeems every tear.

So, as you close this final chapter, may you open a new one in your life—with boldness, with clarity, and with the unshakeable faith that moves every giant that attempts to rise against you in your life. All this time the brokenness was never beyond repair. You were becoming. Keep rising. Keep healing. Keep becoming her—*the one you were always destined to be.*

SIS... Get Up!

THE WORDS I NEVER SAID... THE HEALING I'M READY TO RECEIVE.

Take a deep breath. Place your hand over your heart.

Now ask yourself: What am I still carrying that I've never spoken out loud?

There are wounds so silent, even language feels inadequate. But healing doesn't always begin with words—it begins with truth.

In your journal today, write a letter to:

The version of you that didn't know how to ask for help.

The people who broke your heart or betrayed your trust (even if you never send it).

The you of today—standing on the edge of a new beginning.

....

....

....

....

....

....

....

....

....

....

....

....

....

evolve

Sometimes, IT. IS. YOU. Do the work: heal, elevate, <u>evolve</u>, learn and GET UP!

STEPHANIE P. GREEN

SPECIAL THANKS

• • •

On my journey, there were pivotal individuals in my life who helped me to GET UP. I would like to take a moment to thank each of them:

- Rosa Lee Tucker Kirby
- Suffragan Bishop Leonia Palmer
- Bishop R.C. Blakes, Jr.
- Pastor James D. Edwards
- LPC Shavon Bailey
- Minister Lisa Logan
- Minister Frances Mosley

Each of these individuals on my journey of healing has been a powerful force and voice of strength and resounding encouragement.

I give special honor to Jesus Christ. He allowed me to keep a sound mind, made me unrecognizable (mentally, spiritually, physically, and emotionally), strengthened every area of my life, and allowed me to come out better and not bitter. There is no gain without pain. Pain pays, but it is our choice to decide how we receive the compensation. There was no way that after all the battles God allowed me to live through, I was choosing anything other than life. Sis, GET UP and LIVE—choose purpose, choose life, and choose YOU. I love you.

I feel prompted to say: Many times when a prophecy, a Word, or a declaration of blessings is made over someone's life, and if our name is not specifically called, we can overlook the Call or think, "He/she wasn't talking to me." (Insert your name here), I am speaking directly to you. You are too blessed and have survived too many hardships to abandon yourself, to turn back, and renounce the dedication you've worked so hard for. I am a living witness and evidence—you will succeed.

I have shared practical knowledge inspired by the Spirit of God given to me to give you, to GET UP. I am praying and standing in agreement with you for whatever changes are needed in your life. This I know to be true: The fact that you are still breathing and have read to the end of this book means, Sis, it's not too late—it's the beginning. Peace, Love, & Light.

Your Sister,
Stephanie

ABOUT THE AUTHOR

• • •

Stephanie P. Green is a woman shaped by storms and softened by grace. She is a Licensed Psychotherapist, a gifted actress, and a soulful entrepreneur who walks with purpose and speaks with power. With the heart of a healer and the fire of a survivor, Stephanie doesn't just show up—she *stands up* for those learning to rise.

As the founder of Counseling Services of America, LLC, her calling has taken her across cultures, nationalities and communities—offering a voice to the voiceless and a safe place to land for those carrying heavy hearts. She's just not trained and specializes in mental health—she's *lived* through mental, spiritual, and emotional battles herself. That's what makes her presence different. It's not just therapeutic—it's *transformative.*

Stephanie creates a space where truth can breathe and pain can speak—without shame. Her clients know her not just as a clinician, but as a witness to the wound, and a midwife to healing. Her work blends sound clinical wisdom with soul-deep empathy, reminding each person she meets that broken doesn't mean unworthy and that healing is divine intrinsic work.

Her own life is not polished perfection—it's a beautiful, mosaic pieced together by the hand of God. She has endured betrayal, heartbreak, loss, and the weight of grief, yet she rose—not untouched, but undeniably *anointed.*

You may find her quoting Maya Angelou:

"I'm just trying to be a rainbow in someone else's cloud."

Whether she's sitting in a therapy session, commanding a stage, speaking life through her writing, or building businesses that serve the soul, Stephanie P. Green brings *Peace, Love, and Light* into every space she steps into. And when she leaves, you'll feel a little stronger, a little braver, and a lot more seen.

CONTINUE THE JOURNEY: GRAB THE 'SIS, GET UP WORKBOOK'

• • •

You've read the words, now it's time to *do the work*.

The Sis, Get Up Workbook: 10 Steps to Rise Again is the perfect companion to this book—designed to help you not just read about healing, but *experience* it. With 100 full-color pages (50 guided content + 50 journal pages), this interactive workbook gives you space to reflect, restore, and rise.

Each step includes:

- ∽ Scripture & Daily Devotionals
- ∽ Powerful Affirmations
- ∽ Daily Prayers & Self-Care Prompts
- ∽ Breathwork, Mindfulness & Rest Exercises
- ∽ Therapeutic Tools like the Ikigai Wheel, Emotional Check-Ins & Healing Worksheets
- ∽ 5 Themed Crossword Puzzles
- ∽ 5 Inspirational Coloring Pages
- ∽ Journal Prompt Lists for Every Chapter

❧ Quote Pages Featuring Words from Dr. Sharon Nesbitt and More

You'll work through transformative topics like:

❧ Healing the wounded soul

❧ Rebuilding self-worth

❧ Releasing fear

❧ Setting new standards

❧ Awakening the Queen within

❧ Guarding your power

❧ And becoming whole—mind, body, and spirit.

If this book helped you get up, the workbook will help you *stay up*.

Grab your copy of the *Sis, Get Up Workbook* and step fully into the next chapter of your healing journey.

You were never meant to stay down.

KEEP IN TOUCH

• • •

Stephanie P. Green, LPC, LCMHC

Counseling Services of America

Email: counselingservicesofamerica@gmail.com

Web: www.CounselingServicesofAmerica.com

YouTube Channel: LET'S TALK ABOUT IT WITH STEPHANIE P. GREEN

www.ingramcontent.com/pod-product-compliance
Lightning Source LLC
Chambersburg PA
CBHW060421090426
42734CB00011B/2393